Smarter, Not Harder

Smarter, Not Harder

Sharon Marshall Johnson
with Marita Littauer

Illustrated by Corey Overholtzer

CLASServices Inc.
P.O. Box 66810, Albuquerque, NM 87193, 800-433-6633
www.classervices.com

© Sharon Marshall Johnson

All rights reserved. No part of this book may be reproduced in any form without written permission from CLASServices, P.O. Box 66810, Albuquerque, NM 87193. www.classervices.com

Cover design by Marita Littauer

ISBN 5-559-28192-1

Printed in the United States of America

Table of Contents

Forward by Florence Littauer i

Introduction ii

Popular Sanguine 1

Powerful Choleric 5

Perfect Melancholy 9

Peaceful Phlegmatic 13

Study Theories 17

Personality Profile 18

About the Author 20

Recommended Resources 21

Forward
By Florence Littauer

You have heard the expression; "there is nothing new under the sun." In many ways this is true. It seems like every idea has been thought, every item has been created, and every plan has been developed. Yet, new things are being invented everyday, new products are being produced all the time. Some of these introductions are totally new; others are an improvement on an existing idea — making them seem totally new.

Smarter, Not Harder falls into the latter category. The basic ideas of the four personalities has been around for over 2000 years and was originally discovered by the Greek philosopher Hippocrates. In the years since then, many people have benefited from his original ideas. They found that understanding their personality and the personality of others helped them get along better. In recent years, life has become much more complex and people have found one of their biggest struggles in life is in their relationships. Therefore the concepts Hippocrates created have taken on à renewed popularity. They have been taught in schools, colleges and businesses — sometimes using the original Greek words Hippocrates created: Sanguine, Choleric, Melancholy and Phlegmatic, sometimes using different modern terms, and sometimes — as we have done, a combination of the Greek and modern words.

I first came in contact with this teaching over 30 years ago. As I learned about my personality, my eyes were opened. Understanding who I was, and the personality type of others, improved my married life and my parenting skills. My children learned about their own personality and found that understanding their strengths and weaknesses helped them in school. They got along better with their friends and teachers.

I have been teaching, speaking and writing on this subject for years, however my focus has been primarily on adults. While I used to be a schoolteacher, I never presented The Personalities to my pupils. However, Sharon Marshall Johnson has adapted the material for students. For the last twenty years she has been working with middle and high school students through the SCORE program and has seen amazing changes when young people begin to see that just because someone is different doesn't make him wrong. I am so excited that Sharon has taken her expertise on this subject and put it together in a time-tested treatment that students can quickly understand, grasp and use to make a difference in their relationships both at home and at school.

When you read and study this booklet, you will find that this material will help you to work **Smarter, Not Harder!**

Florence Littauer
Speaker/Author
Silver Boxes, Personality Plus

Introduction

Dear Parents:

I am so grateful that when I entered jr. high school I understood the basic concepts in this book. Knowing what my strengths and weaknesses were helped me capitalize on my strengths at school. Since I am a Popular Sanguine, and have always been a talker, but have never been much of a detail person, I offered to give my reports orally rather than in a written format. My teachers were so thrilled that I was willing to give an oral report that they readily accepted my proposal. I got extra credit for the oral report and didn't get graded on my areas of weakness — spelling and punctuation.

Understanding my teachers' personalities helped me know which ones I could joke around with and with which ones I had better toe the line. This helped my grades and made the entire school experience more pleasant for everyone. The sooner children learn about their personality, the quicker they can begin to benefit from that knowledge.

For years my mother and I have been teaching and writing on the subject of The Personalities. Because they found the teaching to be so helpful, the adults at our seminars and conferences often ask, "Do you have anything for youth?" "Is there anything we can take home for our teenagers?" While young people usually can grasp the basic ideas from the books **Personality Plus**, **Personality Puzzle** and **Getting Along With Almost Anybody** and we get reports that they enjoy the audio tapes on the subject, we have not had anything specifically for their unique needs — until now!

Smarter, Not Harder is written in a clear and easy to read fashion. If your children do not already know their personality, have them start by taking the personality profile at the end of this booklet. It was specifically created for middle and high school students, although many younger students find they have no trouble with it. As they answer the questions, encourage them to think about how they really feel about themselves rather than what you or their teachers might want them to be. Once they have identified their own personality, they should read the section that applies to them. They should read about their primary personality first and then if they have a strong secondary personality type, they should also read that section. Once they have an understanding of their own Personality, they will enjoy reading through the other sections as well. The practical advice in each section will help students maximize their personality strengths and minimize their weaknesses both at home and school, with their teachers, friends and even with you! Our experience has been that they will talk about themselves in a real way when they are given this opportunity. You can hardly sit down and say, "What do you think about yourself?" But, when you use the Personality Profile as an opener, it is amazing what they begin to talk about.

Giving your child this booklet is one of the most helpful things you can do to help them go through school, and their life, **Smarter, Not Harder!**

Marita Littauer
President, CLASServices Inc.

Dear Student,

Have you noticed how some people can talk forever without saying anything?

Do you study all the time, but the person sitting beside you goofing off gets the good grades...and it's just not fair!?

Do you have teachers who really know their stuff, but they're boring...boring...boring?

Have you noticed that some of the teachers you think are great your friends don't like at all?

Sometimes, do your friends (or parents) get their feelings hurt over seemingly stupid things?

Have you ever wondered why you can tell a joke one time and have people howling with laughter; but when you tell the same joke to another group, no one thinks it's funny?

You'll understand all these things and more when you learn about The Personalities.

There's only one of you!

They say your **temperament** is what you're born with; your **personality** is how you express it; and **character** is what you do with it.

Through the profile at the end of this book, you can learn what you were born with. Through the pointers throughout these pages, you can learn how to express your personality more effectively. As you take responsibility for your life, develop your many good qualities, offset your weaknesses, and learn from your mistakes, you will refine your character.

Oh...did I mention it will take you a lifetime? But...the journey will be better, more fun, smoother, and more productive if you build a solid foundation. That is what this book is all about.

You're in charge!

Victor, a ninth grader came to me irate. "I've got an awful, rotten, racist teacher, and I hate him. I'm going to sit in his class and fail and do nothing!"

We talked about his teacher, and I agreed. If what he told me was true, I wouldn't like the guy either! But what he said had an inherent problem...if he failed the class, he would have to take it again next year, but the teacher would still get paid. In short, the teacher wins; Victor loses. We call that "stinkin' thinkin'".

The first character-building lesson we learn is that we, not our teacher, are responsible for our education. Our teacher doesn't use a can opener to open our head and pour the knowledge in; we must search for it. Since it is our responsibility, we learn better when we learn to communicate with our teacher and make others our partners rather than our opponents. We have to learn to ask questions, go the extra mile, and challenge low grades without threatening the teacher's authority.

"If what you told me is true," I continued, "he probably doesn't like you either. He would be pleased to see you fail. Make him give you an A! It'll drive him crazy!"

Victor took my advice and let us help him learn "smart, rather than hard." By the time he earned his A, he had also earned a great partner in his education. He and his teacher actually liked one another!

Know what you need, and build your life around it.

"I want to be a cosmetologist," she told me. Looking at her perfect makeup and hair, I assured her she had a natural talent that would help her succeed. I asked about her personality type. That, too, affects how we will negotiate our chosen careers. She was a Powerful Choleric. Soon you'll learn that Powerful Cholerics are straight shooters. They don't mince words; they don't get their feelings hurt easily; they tell it like it is.

"Red flag!," I said. "Powerful Cholerics don't enjoy listening to people's problems, and about 80% of a cosmetologist's job is listening to sob stories as they work on someone's hair. We need to set you up with a business background so you can also own the shop."

Her response? "I really want to be an attorney, but I didn't think you'd believe me."

Attorney or cosmetologist? The choice is yours! But whatever you do in life, make sure it fulfills you. Life is too short to spend that much time in something you're not passionate about! Listen to who you are and what you need to be fulfilled. Prepare for a career that matches it.

Work Smarter, Not Harder!

In a news special, Peter Jennings redefined "smart": "A smart person is someone who knows what they're good at and who knows what they're not good at. They capitalize on their strengths and they compensate for their weaknesses."

In Mrs. Rose's English class (Visalia, CA), one of her students handed in an unfinished paper. Since they had studied about personalities, she thought a note was in order. She wrote, "Since I'm a Popular Sanguine, I didn't finish." Mrs. Rose wrote back, "Since I'm a Powerful Choleric, you get an F."

I don't think that's quite what Peter Jennings had in mind!

This booklet will help you capitalize on your strengths and compensate for your weaknesses. First, learn your strengths and celebrate them. Get better at them. Think about how you feel, what you accomplish, and how you interact with others when you work in your strengths; probably you're energized and happy when a job is finished.

Next, take an honest look at your weaknesses. A strength carried to excess becomes a weakness. Don't waste any time hating yourself for what you're not...and don't make excuses for your weaknesses; that paralyzes you, and you get weaker. Instead, use the tips in this booklet to learn how to compensate for them.

I bet you didn't know it was that easy to be smart!

May your life be rich and full. May your greatest dreams come true. I entrust my future to you, the next generation...and I know it will be good!

Sharon Marshall Johnson, Director
SCORE: Success in the CORE for Everyone!
sharonmarjo@earthlink.net

POPULAR SANGUINE

You're a Popular Sanguine and that's good! Being a Popular Sanguine means you're creative, enthusiastic, and willing to take risks. As you learn to know yourself, like yourself, and develop your strengths, you'll be able to achieve your goals and reach your dreams. As you learn how to interact with other people who think and view the world differently, you'll be able to enjoy life even more. You're such a complex, creative person that it will take a lifetime to explore your own mind, but a few simple hints will help you as you work with others.

To get along better in a classroom, remember:

- You need excitement and spontaneity to keep your interests alive. If you're in a class that's boring to you, make your teacher think it's your favorite. Teachers like that, and you're good at enthusiasm. See how many ways you can find to do this (i.e. ask questions, smile and give eye contact to the teacher during discussions, take creative class notes, etc.).

- You need to create excitement and spontaneity in your classes in a quiet way (which is difficult for your personality). If you're artistic, try adding creativity and spontaneity by drawing pictures of the concepts being presented by the teacher. (Make sure you explain your notes to your teacher ahead of time, though. Otherwise your teacher might think you're not paying attention.) If you're great with words, while you take notes, see how many synonyms you can find for a key point the teacher is expressing. In other words, make a game of listening actively and quietly. Some teachers will provide you with an outlet for your creativity. In other classrooms, to get along well with the teacher, you need to become creative in silent ways (that may or may not eventually be shared with the rest of the class).

- You live in the present. When a teacher gives an interesting assignment, you're always quick to volunteer. Remember since you're "now-oriented," you'll forget the assignment and/or your commitment to it when you walk out of the classroom. In fact, you could stand in front of your locker trying to decide what books to take home and convince yourself you don't even have any homework..."out of sight is out of mind". Keep an assignment sheet. Be sure you write down everything you volunteer for, with the deadlines, and check your assignment sheet before you go home each day.

To learn "smarter, not harder:"

- Create stories to help you remember what you're trying to learn.

- See how many ways you can solve the same problem.

- Have contests with your friends to keep you motivated.
- Study with friends. You automatically see the practical application of a concept. Your friends can help you discover the breadth, depth, and the end result.
- Act out assignments.
- Use a tape recorder and talk through your assignments. Because of your natural spontaneity and your gift with words, you often learn with your mouth open. Sometimes you say things that don't make sense in the process of trying to understand. Then all of a sudden, an amazing concept will come out of your mouth. Because you live in the present, you forget that idea about as quickly as you speak it. If you keep a tape recorder handy, you can go back and recapture those tidbits (and erase all the mindless chatter that got you to the point).

To better communicate with your friends:

- Become an active listener. Your superior ability with words sometimes causes you to interrupt your friends before they finish what they are saying. Instead, try listening and then repeating back to them what they said before you go into your response.
- When you're involved in a group discussion, write down your ideas so you won't forget them. Then wait for other people to bring up what you were thinking before you talk about a topic. In other words, make a game of being quiet so you don't dominate the discussion.
- Remember, as much as you dislike structure, some of your friends need it. Occasionally give in and agree to their scheduled activities. At other times, teach them to be more spontaneous and take risks along with you.
- Again, remember you live in the present. To remember important things and dates, like birthdays and assignments, write yourself notes.

To get along with your parents:

- Share your dreams and goals with them.
- Listen to the dreams and goals they have for you.
- Try to cooperate with them rather than fighting. You'll enjoy life more and go further if you and your parents play on the same team rather than competing with one another and becoming rivals.

- When you disagree, try to understand the reasons for their opinions. Also try to understand, and help them understand, why you feel the way you do about a decision. Sometimes it helps to depersonalize the impact of a disagreement when you write it down before talking about it. Keep your conversation a discussion, not a confrontation.
- Learn as much as you can about their primary personalities. When you understand why or whether they get their feelings hurt easily or need "all the facts" before they make decisions, you can accommodate them easier.

To get along better with your teachers:

If you understand what your teacher needs based on personality style, you'll be able to meet those needs and improve your grades. Once you understand personalities, you'll usually be able to spot what personality each teacher is. If you don't know you might ask some friends in your class or begin listening or watching from a different perspective.

If a teacher is Powerful Choleric, that teacher will give you all the perimeters of an assignment up front. You'll know specifically what your teacher is trying to accomplish with the lesson, what you need to learn, how you need to do it, and the steps you need to take to get there.

To get along better with Powerful Choleric teachers:

- Remember Powerful Choleric teachers are what we call "bottom liners." That means they always keep the goal in mind. A Powerful Choleric teacher doesn't like someone deviating from the goal. Your creative sense of humor sometimes will be viewed as a distraction, and your teacher may feel you don't take lessons seriously. You do need some spontaneity and creativity in your life. But remember, if you have a teacher who is Powerful Choleric, try to keep the humor focused on the end result and on the process.

- Powerful Choleric teachers want assignments completed, they want them done well, they want them turned in on time, and they want their directions followed. In the middle of being you and being creative, be sure that you stay focused on the subject.

If your teacher is a Popular Sanguine, you can expect some story-telling in the classroom and maybe some deviation from the lesson with jokes or something funny. Your Popular Sanguine teachers will do a lot of group activities and will not give you much quiet time — Popular Sanguines don't like quiet.

To get along better with Popular Sanguine teachers:

- Remember that even though they enjoy a good laugh and a good joke, they need to be center stage. You want to be enthusiastic about what they're presenting, but you don't want to take over the class and upstage them.

- A Popular Sanguine teacher will appreciate you using your imagination.

- A Popular Sanguine teacher will appreciate your practical ideas.

- A Popular Sanguine teacher will appreciate your enthusiasm. Make sure it shows.

If your teacher is a Perfect Melancholy, your teacher will dig deeply into assignments. The teacher will like looking at symbolism, names, dates, and places. The teacher will like making connections regarding an issue. For example, in literature, a Perfect Melancholy teacher would dig deeply into the story — "Joe said this, which caused so and so to do this, which caused so and so to do this," and draw conclusions from the depth. A Perfect Melancholy teacher will expect and appreciate details in all assignments.

To get along better with Perfect Melancholy teachers:

- Remember that you intuitively approach learning from an entirely different perspective than that of a Perfect Melancholy teacher. The Perfect Melancholy teacher sees depth, names, dates, and places. You could read a passage and not even see a name, date, and place because your mind is spinning about possibilities, opportunities, and practical application. Ask for help in knowing what's important to that teacher.

- Often if you tell a joke in a Perfect Melancholy teacher's classroom, you hurt that teacher's feelings. The teacher will think you're shallow and don't really care about the material. You need to develop skills, then watch a teacher's reaction to your sense of humor. If the reaction is negative, don't repeat it. Make a personal connection to show your interest by asking well-thought-out questions.

- Study with a friend who's Perfect Melancholy, so you can help that friend with application and that friend can help you see the detail that your mind just naturally overlooks.

If a teacher is a Peaceful Phlegmatic, that teacher will likely look at the big picture and give you lots of options about approaching a topic. Instead of digging deep into the story, your Peaceful Phlegmatic teacher will likely look at it from a variety of viewpoints and then say, "This is how you can use it in life; this is how we see it in nature, etc."

Peaceful Phlegmatics look at applications from many different perspectives and at meanings behind the application. Peaceful Phlegmatics look at human relationships in any lesson.

To get along better with Peaceful Phlegmatic teachers:

- Connect with the teachers at a personal level.

- Peaceful Phlegmatic teachers will enjoy your sense of humor as long as it doesn't hurt someone's feelings or make that person look foolish or incompetent.

- Although their classes may be passive, they will include activities if they know you enjoy them, so suggest them — but in an excited way, not as a "put down."

- They will work hard to please you as long as you communicate that you value them as people and make a personal connection. Ask them how they feel about something. Write down personal things they mention (like family and birthdays) so you'll remember to ask about them later.

Lots of great and accomplished people are "Popular" Sanguine:

- Former President Ronald Reagan
- Simon Peter from the Bible
- Jenna Elfin from Darma & Greg
- President Bill Clinton
- Actor Jim Carrey
- Actor Lucile Ball (I Love Lucy)

Remember, all these good things about you, carried to excess, can become your weaknesses.

For example, your superior ability to be spontaneous and creative when telling a story, carried to excess, can cause you to forget the truth. Your need to be free, carried to excess, can result in a lack of some needed discipline in your life. Keep your life in balance.

When choosing your career, consider your needs, your strengths, and your weaknesses. You need an audience. You need to have some control over how you spend your time. You need a job where you can use your creativity. You need to interact with people.

POWERFUL CHOLERIC

You're a Powerful Choleric and that's good! Being Powerful Choleric means you're goal oriented. You know your mind, and you're willing to take risks. As you learn to know yourself, like yourself, and develop your strengths, you'll be able to achieve your goals and dreams. As you learn how to interact with other people who think and view the world differently, you'll be able to control your world and enjoy your life even more. You're such a complex, creative person that it will take a lifetime to understand you. A few simple hints will help you as you work with others.

To get along better in a classroom, remember:

- You need to know where you're going. If you're in a class where a teacher appears disorganized or shallow, you have a tendency to act out or take over, which may get your into trouble. Sometimes your honest question, "Where are we headed with this?" is misconstrued to be a challenge to authority. The end result is a battle instead of an answer. Remember, although you enjoy a good argument, most teachers don't. And right or wrong, the teachers are the ones in charge in a classroom.

- Develop active listening skills to keep you from alienating your teachers. To put your intolerance on hold for a few minutes, you might approach your classes as if you were teaching them. As you listen to each teacher beat around the bush and explain things from multiple perspectives, you might try, in your class notes, designing your own lesson (pretend you're the teacher). Create your own agenda by listening, reacting, and thinking about the end result and goal orientation on paper. This process will enable you to become an active listener and will channel some of your creative energy into the "waiting game," — waiting for the teacher to get around to mentioning the bottom line. It is, of course, appropriate for you to know the end result and the goal orientation; but you need to hone your communication skills in the process of learning them.

- You value concepts and end results more than you do facts and details. This means when you're in a classroom with a teacher who is detail oriented, you can become impatient. However, because you are goal-oriented, once you decide to learn facts and details (by reading a teacher to know it's important to that person), you can quickly acquire them. You might create a game of learning the concepts.

- You usually believe you could teach the class yourself so you may find sitting still a bit tedious. Develop the habit of becoming an active learner. Take notes, and use your creative thoughts to reinforce learning while you're sitting there.

- Ask if you can help teach a lesson.

- Ask if you can tutor others in the class, who are struggling to learn.

To learn "smarter, not harder":

- Develop active listening techniques. Being goal oriented, it's easy for you to zoom right past the sub-points to the bottom line. However, in many classrooms, that ability gets you into trouble. You might develop the art of giving feedback (paraphrasing what someone just said). Also, make sure you listen to all the details before you jump in.

- Create a game and/or competition out of what you're attempting to learn.

- Study with friends. Although you have the ability to conquer almost any subject alone, studying with friends will help you view assignments from multiple perspectives. You naturally see the end result. Your friends can help you see the "big picture," the microscope viewpoint, and practical applications.

- Walk, dance, or move as you study. Your inability to sit still can cause frustration as you complete assignments. Developing the ability to move while you think about multiple things at once can help you focus.

To better communicate with your friends:

- Paraphrase back to them what you heard them say. So often friends think of you as not being a good listener. You can be with just a few techniques. Before responding, develop the habit of saying, "So what you're saying is…" and repeating it back in different words. When your friends know you heard them, they're more apt to listen to what you have to say — and you always have an idea worth sharing!

- Develop the habit of asking questions rather than giving responses. Your quick ability to see an end result can cause you to be a harsh judge of friends. Although you're usually right, friends appreciate and learn from the opportunity to come to their own decisions. Ask leading questions, rather than telling them what to do (for example, rather than saying, "You should dump the creep for treating you this way," say, "What do you really want in your friendships? Is this person treating you with the respect that you deserve? If not, what do you think you should do?"). This leads them to the same conclusion you would have given but is gained by choice rather than decree.

- Schedule time for friends. Remember that your busy life and your high energy in creating projects and achieving goals can pull you away from relationships. Take the time to interact with people.

To get along with your parents:

- Share your dreams and goals with them.

- Listen to their dreams and goals for you. Discuss how the two are different. Remember, you have the right to make your own decisions, but your parents love you and also want what's good for you. The more you can share with one another, the better you'll get along.

- Remember they are the parents. Your goal orientation and ability to take charge sometimes causes you to challenge their authority. Negotiate for what part of the household you'll control, but don't take the whole thing over.

To help you get along better with your teachers:

If you understand what each teacher needs based on personality style, you'll be able to meet those needs and improve your grades. Once you understand personalities, you'll usually be able to spot which one your teacher is. If you don't know you might ask some friends in your class or begin listening and watching from a different perspective.

If a teacher is a Powerful Choleric, you usually know all the perimeters of an assignment up front. You know specifically what that person is trying to accomplish with the lesson, what you need to learn, how you need to do it, and the steps it will take to get there.

To get along better with Powerful Choleric teachers:

- You'll need to remember that two strong-willed people who need control share the classroom. By nature of the job, the Powerful Choleric teacher has the right to control so be sure you don't get involved in a power struggle.

- Find something you can control while you respect the authority of the classroom teacher.

If you have a Popular Sanguine teacher, you can expect some story-telling in the classroom and maybe some deviation from the lesson with jokes or something funny. Your Popular Sanguine teachers will do a lot of group activities and will not give you much quiet time (they don't like quiet).

To get along better with Popular Sanguine teachers:

- You may have a tendency to take over the class. Don't! Whether they sound organized or not, they don't like to be upstaged.

- Remember that your Popular Sanguine teacher needs to be center stage and thrives on a positive audience reaction. Be careful that your need to move toward a goal isn't misread by your teacher as a depreciation of, or an attempt to, upstage him or her.

If you find a negative reaction to your questions, you might ask another person to ask your questions. This gets your needs met without you appearing offensive. In the process, you can learn how to ask questions tactfully (DO: "Mrs. Jones, can you please explain the significance of the end of the cold war on this issue?" DON'T: "Why do we have to discuss this? Everybody knows the cold war is over").

If your teacher is a Perfect Melancholy, your teacher will dig deeply into assignments. The teacher will like looking at symbolism, names, dates, and places. The teacher will like making connections about an issue. For example, in literature a Perfect Melancholy teacher would dig deeply into the story — "Joe said this, which caused so and so to do this, which caused so and so to do this," and draw conclusions from the depth. A Perfect Melancholy teacher will expect and appreciate details in all assignments.

To get along better with Perfect Melancholy teachers:

- You'll likely have your need for structure and depth met. Remember, though, that Perfect Melancholies take a longer time to get to the end result than you're comfortable with. You might create a diversion for yourself to help you sit still while you tune in to the depth, process, and discussions of your Perfect Melancholy teacher. Sometimes keeping your hands busy allows you to sit still and focus. You might try taking some creative notes, i.e., writing little notes to yourself on the side of your class notes, coming up with conclusions, second guessing the teacher, etc.

- Perfect Melancholies tend to get their feelings hurt easily if they don't feel they are valued. Make sure that your questions are couched with care so they come across as honest questions rather than confrontation (i.e., "I'm kind of lost. How does a study of food relate to Puritan culture," rather than, "So what does food have to do with it?")

If your teacher is a Peaceful Phlegmatic, your teacher will likely look at the gestalt, at the big picture, and give you lots of options about approaching something. Instead of digging deep into the story, your Peaceful Phlegmatic teacher will likely take a look at a story and then say, "Now, this is how you can use it in life; this is how we see it in nature, etc." Peaceful Phlegmatics look at applications from many different perspectives and at meanings behind the application. Peaceful Phlegmatics look at human relationships in any lesson.

To get along better with Peaceful Phlegmatic teachers:

- Find something to keep your hands busy, to help you sit still and focus. Phlegmatic teachers build in reflection time, thinking time, and relationship time. These are not things that you innately need. You may view this time as lacking focus. If you do, you have a tendency to take over the class. This creates a power struggle and doesn't result to your benefit, the teacher's benefit, or the benefit of the other students. Back away from this power struggle and create other ways to keep your mind occupied.

- Remember that the Peaceful Phlegmatic needs relationship. When you ask bottom-line questions, the Peaceful Phlegmatic feels as though you're challenging that relationship and devaluing him or her as a person. For that reason, develop skills of couching your questions (i.e., writing your questions out, asking your questions one-on-one after class, etc.). You do have the right to have your need for goal-orientation met, but learn to develop people skills as you meet your own needs.

Lots of great and accomplished people are Powerful Cholerics:

- Former President Richard Nixon
- The Apostle Paul from the Bible
- Actress Whoopi Goldberg
- First Lady Hilary Clinton
- Secretary of State Madeleine Albright
- Actor/Singer Frank Sinatra
- Attorney General Janet Reno
- Radio personality Rush Limbaugh

Remember, all these good things about you, carried to excess, can become your weaknesses.

For example, your superior ability to be decisive and take charge, when carried to excess, can cause you to forget about another person's right to an opinion and to a decision different from your own or others may see you as bossy. Your need for knowledge and power, when carried to excess, can sometimes cause you to forget about truth in important areas in life. Keep your life in balance.

When choosing your career, consider your needs, your strengths, and your weaknesses. You need to have your intelligence respected. You need to have control over how you spend your time and the ability to make decisions.

PERFECT MELANCHOLY

You're a Perfect Melancholy and that's good! Being a Perfect Melancholy means you have a strong sense of order, fairness, and responsibility. It also means you're able to see the deep core issues in any situation — you don't just look at the surface. As you learn to know yourself, like yourself, and develop your strengths, you'll be able to achieve your goals and dreams. As you learn how to interact with other people, who think and view the world differently, you'll be able to order your world and enjoy life even more. You're a complex, creative person and it will take a lifetime to understand you. A few simple hints will help you as you work with others.

To get along better in a classroom, remember:

- You need depth when you study. With that in mind, you get along well in most classes — unless you're in a class with a teacher who appears disorganized. When you end up with such a teacher, you need to take on that organizational task for yourself. Structure your class notes, and check on details with a friend or teacher at the end of each class or day.

- When your needs aren't met, you often take it personally. Teachers who cover material in a practical (rather than deep) way often hurt your feelings when you ask them questions (Remember, they don't mean to hurt you and usually aren't aware they have). You'll need to learn to approach them one-on-one instead of in large groups. You might write down key points as you listen in class and develop the habit of checking after class with the teacher and/or a group of friends to fill in details. Remember, you do have the right to understand an assignment and understand the material from a depth perspective. You may need to meet these needs one-on-one if you find your in-class questions aren't taken seriously.

- You operate well with schedules and lists. Be sure you keep an assignment sheet and develop a weekly calendar for your studies. You'll accomplish more if you develop a routine, setting aside the same time every day for homework, reading, studying, and review.

- You have a tendency to be a perfectionist, and there's never enough time to finish everything according to your standards. You'll need to learn to prioritize! Prior to studying, set some realistic time frames for your work. Develop the habit of giving it creative energy during that time frame and quitting when you've committed the right amount of time to a project, even though it isn't finished to your satisfaction. Remember that your deep need for perfection can cause you to turn in assignments late, thus lowering your grades. You'll have to make some personal choices based on what topics are of deep enough interest to you to merit you putting in the extra time.

To learn "smarter, not harder:"

- Develop the habit of complementing yourself. You're a serious, deep learner; but you seek approval. Learn to ask for feedback, and learn to tell yourself what you do well.
- Always take notes in class. This will help you focus. It will also give you a tool to curb your frustration level while you attempt to understand a disorganized teacher.
- Study with friends of different personality types. Your genius in areas of depth and detail will compliment another person's genius in the area of looking at the big picture, goal, or practical application. You can learn from one another.
- Draw pictures and make charts and graphs to try to understand the concept at a deeper level. A different perspective will spur you on to greater creativity.
- Try putting your assignment into a different mode. For example, develop a poem, story, song, rap, picture, or a dance. This helps you get in touch with your creative processes and allows learning to be a more complete experience for you.
- Set realistic time limits prior to beginning an assignment. Don't spend so much time in getting ready that you have no time to do the work.

To better communicate with your friends:

- Develop your active listening skills, i.e. restate what another person said, asking if you understood. Because of your sensitive nature, sometimes you get your feelings hurt and your friends don't even know they've said anything to offend you. If you develop active listening skills, you'll be able to tell them what you think you heard them say and gain their responses to make sure you really are communicating. The better you develop your active listening skills, the more you'll be able to enjoy your role as a friend.
- Remember, you need time alone, and that's okay. When you find yourself feeling drained or depressed in a group, pull away and spend some time reading, meditating, exercising, or doing whatever you need to fill you up again. You tend to spend energy in a crowd, whereas some personalities draw energy from a crowd. That means you'll be fresher at the beginning of an evening than the end, so take some time out for you.
- Schedule times for spontaneity. Because you live your life by time blocks and schedules, it's sometimes difficult for you to relax and have fun. Schedule time for fun. Scheduling time to interact with friends will relieve you of the pressure of your inner time clock.
- Try to develop four ways of looking at something: depth (which you're very good at), breadth (the "big picture"), goal orientation (the end result; the bottom line), and practical application (How do I do this? What does it mean to me? How can I apply it in my daily life?) Often when you see your friends as being shallow, it's because they're looking at the goal or the broad picture when you're looking at depth. You'll communicate more effectively and even understand the depth better if you look at the whole concept.

To get along better with your parents:

- Share your dreams and goals with them. Often they don't support you because they don't know what you really want. You tend to be private; but when you risk, you'll usually find support.

- Help them share their dreams and goals for you. You have a tendency to look at your weaknesses and shortcomings. Your parents probably look at your strengths instead. You may be surprised at what they see in you that you don't even know is there.

- Express to them your need for structure. Let them know your schedule ahead of time, and plan with them to schedule family time into your busy day.

If you find yourself disempowered and unable to express yourself, try writing what you'd like to say. Your deep respect for authority sometimes causes you to be unable to express yourself, whereas putting something down on paper helps you think. If you need to discuss something controversial with your parents, you might try writing it out before you talk it out. You might also try rehearsing what you want to say to a teddy bear, the family dog, or a friend if you find emotions get in the way when you're talking to your parents.

To get along better with your teachers:

If you understand what your teachers need based on personality styles, you'll be able to meet those needs and improve your grades. Once you understand personalities, you'll usually be able to spot what each teacher is. If you don't know you might ask some friends in your class or begin listening and watching from a different perspective:

If your teacher is a Popular Sanguine, you can expect some story-telling in the classroom and maybe some deviation from the lesson with jokes or something funny. Your Popular Sanguine teachers will do a lot of group activities and will not give you much quiet time.

To get along better with Popular Sanguine teachers:

- Keep in mind the Popular Sanguine teacher doesn't intend to hurt you. You may be frustrated in the classroom because it seems so disorganized. It may be hard for you to see the purpose of class activities or understand the structure. When you ask questions, a Popular Sanguine teacher who doesn't understand personalities may snap back a funny answer that causes the class to laugh. That embarrasses you and hurts your feelings. The Popular Sanguine teacher gains creativity through humor; keep in mind this response was intended to energize and amuse, not to hurt.

If a teacher is a Perfect Melancholy, your teacher will dig deeply in assignments. The teacher will like looking at symbolism, names, dates, and places. The teacher will like making connections about an issue. For example, in literature a Perfect Melancholy teacher would dig deeply into the story — "Joe said this, which caused so and so to do this, which caused so and so to do this," and draw conclusions from the depth. A Perfect Melancholy teacher will expect and appreciate details in all assignments.

To get along better with Perfect Melancholy teachers:

- You probably will have your need for depth and structure met within the classroom. Your problem will be trying to meet deadlines and come to closure on projects

If a teacher is a Peaceful Phlegmatic, your teacher will likely look at the gestalt, at the big picture, and give you lots of options about approaching something. Instead of digging deeply into the story, your Peaceful Phlegmatic teacher will likely take a look at a story and then say, "Now, this is how you can use it in life; this is how we see it in nature, etc." Peaceful Phlegmatics look at applications from many different perspectives. Peaceful Phlegmatics look at human relationships in any lesson.

To get along better with Peaceful Phlegmatic teachers:

- You may have trouble focusing. Peaceful Phlegmatics tend to look at the big picture rather than depth. Try a creative version of note taking such as a mind map (putting the main idea in the middle and all of the sub-topics out to the side). That way you will stay focused on the topic as you try to understand how the different viewpoints lead toward that central theme.

- Remember that Peaceful Phlegmatic teachers need relationships, so your personal connection with the teacher in any number of ways will help you in the class.

If a teacher is Powerful Choleric, you usually know all the perimeters of an assignment up front. You know specifically what that person is trying to accomplish with the lesson, what you need to learn, how you need to do it, and the steps it will take to get there.

To get along better with Powerful Choleric teachers:

- Remember that Powerful Cholerics see the goal and the fastest way to reach the goal; you tend to see depth and sometimes lose sight of a goal. For that reason Powerful Cholerics may cover material too quickly for you. You may need to spend some extra time with friends trying to gain depth in order to meet your deadlines.

- Powerful Choleric teachers tend to be "bottom liners" so work hard to meet deadlines even if you can't finish a project to your standards. If you see that a timeline is unrealistic for you, before you approach the teacher, try blocking it out into a time schedule. If you're specific with what you need and if you can justify it intellectually, the Powerful Choleric teacher will be most understanding and will help you. They tend, however, not to listen if the "I need more time" comes after the fact or if they feel like you're really stalling.

Powerful Cholerics respect someone who speaks up for himself/herself so don't hesitate to ask your honest questions. They don't get their feelings hurt easily and appreciate it when you get to the point.

Lots of great and accomplished people are Perfect Melancholies:

- Former President Jimmy Carter
- Actor/singer Barbara Streisand
- Moses from the Bible
- Microsoft's Bill Gates (and most computer geniuses)
- Vice President Al Gore
- Actor Edward James Olmos

Remember, all these good things about you, carried to excess, can become your weaknesses.

For example, your superior ability to organize, when carried to excess, can cause you to become rigid. Make sure your schedules set you free rather than boxing you in. Your need for depth on an issue can cause you to become a victim of your time schedule. Remember that you are in control, and you need to choose your battles. Develop the ability early to prioritize, to choose, and to say no. Keep your life in balance.

When choosing your career, consider your needs, your strengths...and your weaknesses. You need structure. You need to have some control over how you spend your time. You need some quiet time. You need a job where you can be appreciated for attending to details and always doing work that is high-quality.

PEACEFUL PHLEGMATIC

You're a Peaceful Phlegmatic and that's good! Being a Peaceful Phlegmatic means you're imaginative, sensitive, compassionate, and a good listener. As you learn to know yourself, like yourself, and develop your strengths, you'll be able to achieve your goals and dreams. As you learn how to interact with other people who think and view the world differently, you'll be able to manage your world and to live a fulfilled life. You're a complex, diverse person and it will take you a lifetime to explore your world, but a few simple hints will help you as you learn to live with others.

To get along better in a classroom, remember:

- Know your mind is diverse. The old saying, "A picture paints a thousand words," certainly applies to you. The teacher can make one statement that sends your mind spinning in dozens of different directions. If you're not especially interested in a class, you can daydream about one of those issues. That means you need to learn to become an active listener to get focused. To do that, take notes in class. In a wide margin of your note page, write the questions that run through your mind so you'll remember to ask them at an appropriate time. Listen to see if the teacher gets around to answering them without you having to ask.

- Learn to take your emotional temperature. Sometimes something happens in class that triggers a feeling. Feelings can also cause you to daydream. Get in touch with your feelings, and jot feelings in the margin of your notes to help make you aware of what is happening in the classroom. In other words, take diverse notes: take notes about the material, about how you feel regarding that material, and about the questions that come to your mind. That will help keep you listening actively and focused on what's being presented.

- Remember that harmonious relationships are important to you. You need to connect at a personal level in order to learn best. With that in mind, it might help you to become acquainted, on a personal level, with your teachers and with your peers. When they become friends and confidants, you'll be more comfortable taking risks and sharing in the classroom.

To learn "smarter, not harder:"

- Find a personal application to the work you're doing ("How can I use this in my music?").

- Look at the whole problem before trying to sort out the details. You've been gifted with the ability to "see the big picture." Once you're comfortable with that, you can zoom in on the specific task at hand.

- Allow yourself time to daydream; use your vivid imagination. Be sure you keep a journal of the thoughts and questions that come up. You often think while you write, so freewrite what comes into your mind to help you solidify what you've learned in a class.

- Study with your friends. While you're gifted in seeing the whole picture, some of your friends will be gifted in picking out details, and others will see practical application or end results. You can learn from one another. Also, you're motivated by being with people in a non-threatening environment. Studying with friends will keep you focused.

- Look for connections in what you're learning. For example, if you read something in literature, think about how it applies to life. Think about where you've heard it in a song. Think about where you've seen it on television. You're good at making connections and can learn by thinking things through.

- Before you begin an assignment, set dates for completing each step. Finishing an assignment or project is difficult for you. This means you could think about an assignment forever without jumping in. You need to set some timelines for yourself.

To better communicate with your friends:

- Make sure they listen when you're speaking. Your easygoing nature and ability to listen well sometimes causes you to be hesitant in sharing your wisdom. When you have something to say, it's usually profound. Get your friends' attention.

- Sometimes you're a little shy when you're trying to express your opinion, so you may enjoy communicating by writing notes to your friends. They'll enjoy receiving personalized notes, and you may be able to better express what you really want to say in writing.

- Get in touch with your values. Your natural flexibility and intuitive ability to understand others' thinking patterns is a gift. Learning what is really important in each area of life will help you develop the ability to make decisions that are best for you. Remember, not making a decision is making a decision.

- You have a unique ability to see talent in other people. Don't hesitate to let them know what you see. Learn to accept their compliments of you and celebrate the great person you are.

To get along with your parents:

- Share your opinions with them. Sometimes because of your quiet, accepting nature, they don't know how you feel or what you think about an issue. When they don't act the way you expect them to, your feelings are hurt. They can't do for you what they didn't know you wanted. Make sure you put your dreams and thoughts into words (perhaps in writing) so they understand.

- Repeat back to them what you heard them say. Sometimes you see the big picture but they're talking about smaller details. In communication, you may not even hear what they intended to say. Develop the art of effective feedback — repeat what you heard them say, then listen to what they say until you understand each other. Otherwise you could talk forever and not accomplish much.

- You don't like conflict. When you disagree with them, watch your reactions. If you shut down emotionally, find a quiet place to write out your thoughts. Go back, paper in hand, to talk to them. Sometimes if you both talk about what you've written (maybe even while you look at the paper instead of one another), your emotions don't get in the way of communication.

To get along better with your teachers:

If you understand what your teachers need based on personality style, you'll be able to meet those needs and improve your grades. Once you understand personalities, you'll usually be able to spot what personality each teacher is. If you don't know you might ask some friends in your classes or begin listening and watching from a different perspective:

If a teacher is a Powerful Choleric, your teacher will give you the goals and details of an assignment up front. You'll know specifically what your teacher is trying to accomplish with the lesson, what you need to learn, how you need to do it, and the steps it will take to get there.

To get along better with Powerful Choleric teachers:

- You may feel somewhat stressed all the time because the Powerful Choleric teacher is goal-oriented and looks at the straightest path to a goal. You are process-and relationship-oriented and need some time for reflection and application. You may need to develop some stress-reduction techniques, i.e., close your eyes and take three deep breaths, journal, take creative notes.
- Build into your homework some time for reflection and application.
- Write in one sentence or less what the focus was of the day's lesson, what you're supposed to do for homework, and how you can use it in your life.

If you find yourself feeling stressed by deadlines and worried about hurting feelings when you ask questions, keep in mind that a Powerful Choleric is a bottom-line person. Powerful Cholerics don't respect people who talk in circles in order to avoid conflict, and they don't get their feelings hurt easily. They will respect a direct question!

If your teacher is a Popular Sanguine, you can expect some story-telling in the classroom and maybe some deviation from the lesson with jokes or something funny. Your sanguine teachers will do a lot of group activities and will not give you much quiet time; Popular Sanguines don't like to be quiet.

To get along better with Popular Sanguine teachers:

- You will probably enjoy classes from the standpoint of subject, diversity, and socialization. Your biggest problem with a Popular Sanguine teacher will be taking the time for reflection to allow you to fully understand a topic. Develop the habit of doing a three minute "splash down" as soon as class is over: reflect and journal for three minutes about the most important topics of the day. That will help you focus in on what the important issues were, finish the topic in your mind, and be ready for something new.
- When you begin your homework assignment, spend a few minutes thinking about the most important issues before you begin so you can focus in on the task at hand.
- Develop the habit of writing, in one sentence or less, the most important thing you learned in class; then write, in one sentence or less, the focus of your homework.

If your teacher is a Perfect Melancholy, your teacher will dig deeply in assignments. Your teacher will like looking at symbolism, names, dates, and places. The Perfect Melancholy teacher will like making connections about an issue. For example, in literature a Perfect Melancholy teacher would dig deeply into the story "Joe said this, which caused so and so to do this, which caused so and so to do this," and draw detailed conclusions. A Perfect Melancholy teacher will expect and appreciate details in all assignments.

To get along better with Perfect Melancholy teachers:

- You will probably have most of your needs met in the course of the classroom in terms of relationships and reflection time. You may have to work to see the big picture because Perfect Melancholy people naturally see depth rather than breadth or application.

- Perfect Melancholy teachers are usually quite receptive to questions that are honest, so don't hesitate to ask questions in class. Just make sure those questions come across as an honest inquiry rather than showing off your incredible dry sense of humor. If the questions come across as humorous, the Perfect Melancholy may think you're playing games and not interested in learning.

If your teacher is a Peaceful Phlegmatic, your teacher will likely look at the big picture and give you lots of options about approaching something. Instead of digging deeply into the story, your Peaceful Phlegmatic teacher will likely take a look at a story and then say, "This is how you can use it in life; this is how we see it in nature," etc. Peaceful Phlegmatics look at applications from many different perspectives and at meanings behind the application. Peaceful Phlegmatics look at human relationships in any lesson.

To get along better with Peaceful Phlegmatic teachers:

- A Peaceful Phlegmatic teacher has the same inner needs that you do: the need for practical application, the need to make a difference in the world, the need to grow at a personal level, and the need to connect with other human beings. Remember to develop a relationship.

Lots of great and accomplished people are Peaceful Phlegmatics:

- Father Abraham from the Bible
- Former President George Bush
- Former President Gerald Ford
- Actor/comedian Drew Carey
- Actor/comedian Jerry Seinfeld
- Chief Joseph, Nez Perce Indian

Remember, all these good things about you, carried to excess, can become your weaknesses.

For example, your superior ability to understand another person's viewpoint and to empathize with your friends, carried to excess, can cause you to compromise your values and beliefs in order to avoid conflict. Your need for harmony and happy relationships, carried to excess, can cause you to pretend that problems don't exist in life. Remember to face the problems because you're very creative in finding solutions. Keep your life in balance.

When choosing your career, consider your needs, your strengths, and your weaknesses. You need to see the "big picture." You need nurturing relationships, and you need to be needed. You might consider jobs that require steady, consistent work instead of high-pressure deadlines.

Regardless of what your personality is, you can learn smarter, rather than harder, by applying these theories of learning to your studies:

1. If you read new information, your brain will remember almost perfectly for about fifteen seconds. Then you will forget fairly rapidly.

2. If you say a fact to yourself over and over again, you will put it in your memory very firmly. This is not the same as re-reading it; it is saying it (and/or writing it).

3. If you ask yourself a question to which the new information is the right answer, then say the new fact to yourself as the answer, this will increase your memory capability.

4. When memorizing facts, material becomes rote after the third repetition. Therefore, rotate material to be memorized in sets of three. The optimum time for memorization is five to fifteen minutes at intervals of two to twenty-four hours.

5. For maximum effectiveness, review should occur between two and twenty-four hours after new material has been introduced.

6. It is easier to remember information if it's associated with something you already know.

7. It is easier to remember new information if you make an absurd association.

8. If you organize new learning in terms of categories, it is easier to remember.

9. If you set up categories before beginning to read, it is easier to notice things that fit into the categories, thus easier to remember.

10. When students know precisely what a teacher expects of them, they are more likely to adjust their behavior to receive the reward and avoid problems.

11. It is best to schedule your studying so that you don't study like subjects in sequence. For example, if you have two subjects that require a large amount of reading comprehension, design a study pattern that places mathematical calculations in between them.

12. Students will tend to study more effectively and avoid burnout if they build refreshing and rewarding breaks into their study periods.

13. The more senses that are involved in the learning process, the more rapidly learning will occur.

14. A student will learn material more thoroughly if asked to explain it to someone else.

15. If material is personalized, it is remembered longer.

Smarter, Not Harder
Youth Personality Profile

Directions: Each statement describes a personality type. Read each statement carefully, check the one in each row across that most often applies to you. If two apply equally, you may check both. Take your totals and place them at the bottom of each appropriate column. The chart on the next page will explain in more detail the characteristics of each personality.

Popular Sanguine	Powerful Choleric	Perfect Melancholy	Peaceful Phlegmatic
I can make any story or joke very funny.	Sometimes people think I mean it, when I am really joking.	I enjoy a good joke, but not when it hurts someone's feelings.	I have a dry sense of humor and can come up with really funny one-liners.
I am excited about the decisions I make. I believe they are good ones.	I like making decisions; I'm usually right.	I want all the facts before I make a decision.	I would rather let others make the decisions.
I like being with others, having fun and being the life of the party.	I enjoy the challenge of being in control when I'm in front of a group.	I enjoy being with people, but I also need time alone.	I go with the flow; I'm comfortable anywhere.
I love to talk more than I like to listen.	When I talk, people listen and pay attention.	I think before I speak so I do not say the wrong thing.	I listen more than I talk so I don't get into trouble.
I make friends easily; people seem to like me.	I like to be in charge when I am with my friends.	I go beyond the surface to discover the real person.	I like to watch people; it gives me a really good picture of what they're like.
I get bored if I have to do the same things all the time. I need excitement.	I like taking on new and daring things because of the challenge.	I keep a schedule so that I know what I am doing next.	I like variety. I like knowing a little bit about a lot of things.
I can come up with really creative ideas that sound like fun.	I like being productive and getting things done quickly.	I'm always analyzing people, places and things.	Sometimes I compromise to avoid conflict.
If I were in a forest, I'd try to find some people; I wouldn't want to be alone.	If I were in a forest, I'd look for the path that would get me out the fastest.	If I were in a forest, I'd examine every detail of a tree, flower, plant or rock. I enjoy nature.	If I were in a forest, I'd see the harmony of how everything fits together; I wouldn't be in a hurry.

Not to be duplicated. See page 22 for ordering information.

Strengths* (see next page)

	Popular Sanguine	Powerful Choleric	Perfect Melancholy	Peaceful Phlegmatic
Emotions	Appealing personality Talkative, storyteller Life of the party Good sense of humor Memory for color Physically holds on to listener Emotional and demonstrative Enthusiastic and expressive Cheerful and bubbling over Curious Good on stage Wide-eyed and innocent Lives in present Changeable disposition Sincere at heart Always a child	Born leader Dynamic and active Compulsive need for change Must right wrongs Strong-willed and decisive Unemotional Not easily discouraged Independent and self-sufficient Exudes confidence Can run anything	Deep and Thoughtful Analytical Serious and purposeful Genius prone Talented and creative Artistic and musical Philosophical and poetic Appreciative of beauty Sensitive to others Self-sacrificing Conscientious Idealistic	Low-key personality Easy going and relaxed Calm, cool and collected Patient, well-balanced Consistent life Quiet and witty Sympathetic and kind Keeps emotions hidden Happily reconciled to life All-purpose person
Work	Volunteers for jobs Thinks up new activities Looks great on the surface Creative and colorful Has energy and enthusiasm Starts in a flashy way Inspires others to join Charms others to work	Goal oriented Sees the whole picture Organizes well Seeks practical solutions Moves quickly to action Delegates work Insists on production Makes the goal Stimulates activity Thrives on opposition	Schedule oriented Perfectionist, high standards Detail conscious Persistent and thorough Orderly and organized Neat and tidy Economical Sees the problems Finds creative solutions Needs to finish what he starts Likes charts, graphs, figures, lists	Competent and Steady Peaceful and agreeable Has administrative ability Mediates problems Avoids conflicts Good under pressure Finds the easy way
Friends	Makes friends easily Loves people Thrives on compliments Seems exciting Envied by others Doesn't hold grudges Apologizes quickly Prevents dull moments Likes spontaneous activities	Has little need for friends Will work for group activity Will lead and organize Is usually right Excels in emergencies	Makes friends cautiously Content to stay in background Avoids causing attention Faithful and devoted Will listen to complaints Can solve other's problems Deep concern for other people Moved to tears with compassion Seeks ideal mate	Easy to get along with Pleasant and enjoyable Inoffensive Good listener Dry sense of humor Enjoys watching people Has many friends Has compassion and concern

Not to be duplicated. See page 22 for ordering information.

*Strengths, when carried to extremes, become weaknesses.

For example:

The **Popular Sanguine** strength of being talkative and a good story teller, when carried to excess, causes the **Popular Sanguine** to exaggerate and sometimes lose sight of truth.

The **Powerful Choleric** strength of being dynamic and active, when carried to excess, causes the **Powerful Choleric** to become a workaholic and mercilessly drive others to achieve.

The **Perfect Melancholy** strength of being analytical, when carried to excess, causes the **Perfect Melancholy** to be critical of others and skeptical of compliments.

The **Peaceful Phlegmatic** strength of being easygoing and relaxed, when carried to excess, causes the **Peaceful Phlegmatic** to avoid responsibility and can sometimes grow into laziness.

About the Author

Sharon Marshall Johnson is the founder and director of SCORE: Success in the SCORE for Everyone. Under her leadership, SCORE grew from a pilot program in Orange County, California to a model program validated by the United States Department of Education. She trains educators throughout the nation to help students work "smarter, not harder."

SCORE works! Students previously in danger of dropping out of school are now graduating and going on to college.

Sharon earned her Bachelor's Degree from Point Loma Nazarene College; her Master of Science from California State University, Fullerton. She directs the Divorce and Grief Recovery program at Crystal Cathedral and is a CLASS speaker. To book Sharon for a keynote address for your organization, contact CLASS at 1-800-433-6633. To learn more about SCORE or to bring SCORE to your school, contact her at Educational Innovations, 30100 Town Center Drive, Suite O-379, Laguna Niguel, CA 92677; 949-363-6764; sharonmarjo@earthlinkl.net, http://home.earthlink.net/~sharonmarjo/

Recommended Resources

For additional reading and study the following resources are recommended

Personality Plus
With over 500,000 copies in print, this is Florence Littauer's most popular book! Her first book on the personalities, *Personality Plus*, will give you an excellent understanding of the four basic personalities. You will gain new understanding of what makes you, your family, and your friends the way they are. Filled with Florence's humorous examples, the strengths and weakness of each personality are thoroughly covered. The popular "Personality Profile" test is included. This book is an excellent basis for a group study.

Personality Plus Tape Set
The famous four-tape series by Florence is still available in this convenient set. These hilarious tapes are packaged with the book and two personality profiles.

Personality Puzzle: Piecing Together the Personalities in Your Workplace
Whether you work in an office, a school, a hospital or even at home, you probably work and come in contact with people who don't see things your way. You may wonder why one is so difficult to get off the phone while another seems almost impolite. Or, why some people accomplish more in times of stress and thrive on change while others appear to freeze when the pressure is on. In *Personality Puzzle* Florence Littauer and Marita Littauer combine their expertise and years of teaching on the personalities to give you a practical guide for understanding the personalities in your workplace. "The Visible Pieces of the Puzzle" will teach you how to identify the personality style of others simply by observing their clothing, body language and workspace. "The Various Pieces" will help you understand each personality type's natural gifts and abilities while "The Valuable Pieces" will show you how to meet the emotional needs of the people at work. If you are the boss or the employee, the client or the co-worker, you can piece together the personalities in your workplace!

Personality Puzzle Audio Tape
An entertaining and educational tape featuring Marita Littauer and her popular teaching on the personalities. Coming from the approach of identifying and understanding the personality types of the people you live and work with, Marita will help you put together the pieces in your Personality Puzzle. You will not only learn to identify each personality type by "The Visible Pieces of the Puzzle," you will gain insight on their various strengths and weaknesses and be able to relate to them in a way to which they will respond the most effectively. This presentation also addresses the various personality combinations and the most common misunderstandings with the personalities.

Personality Profiles

The popular personality test is in each of the books on personality but it is also available by itself. *Updated Profiles*, 6 – 8 1/2 x 11 panels: test, scoring sheet, strengths/weaknesses, word definitions on 2 sides, how to evaluate your scores. *Marketplace Profiles*, 6 – 8 1/2 x 11 panels: same as Updated, but the how-to-evaluate page applies to business and team building. *Youth Version*, 1 – 8 1/2 x11 page, front and back: as found in the back of this booklet. All profiles are full color.

Personality Testing Software

Everything is there – just like on the printed *Personality Profile*: the test, instant scoring, word definitions, strengths and weaknesses. Scores are seen on the screen in bar graph form or can be printed out. Unlimited use! Comes with a 3.5 inch disk, packaged in an attractive album. Great for church, business or home use. Windows 3.1 & 95 compatible.

To order any of these resources or to receive a free book and tape catalog, please call 800/433-6633